To Mukguddu, my father, and Gunballarj and Robyn, my mothers, who gave us this beautiful country and taught us so many things.

And to Esma and Aunty Eileen for all their encouragement and support in this project.

This book is for our wurdurd (children) who love being at Mandilbarreng so much.

DIG, CHOP, SHAKE

Timothy Nabegeyo and children of the Djalama Clan
with Sandra Lees

INDIGENOUS LITERACY FOUNDATION

OH, WE
DIG, DIG, DIG,
AND WE
DIG, DIG, DIG,

HOLD YOUR STICK AND
DIG, DIG, DIG.

WE DIG ALL AROUND FOR
KARRBARDA UNDERGROUND,

WE
DIG, DIG, DIG,
THEY'RE LONG
AND BROWN.

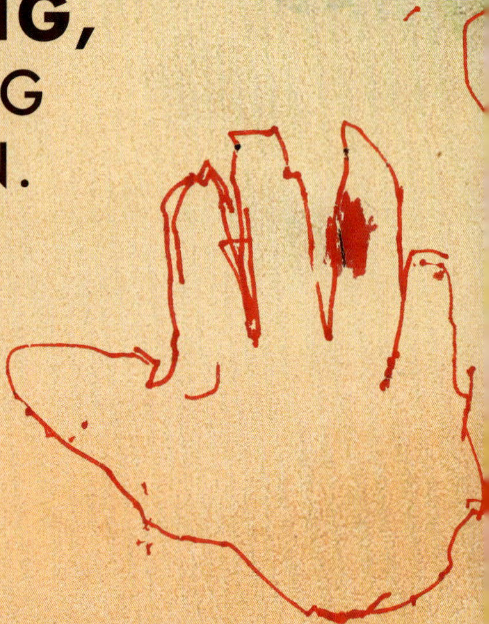

NOW WE
CHOP, CHOP, CHOP,
AND WE
CHOP, CHOP, CHOP,

HOLD YOUR AXE AND
CHOP, CHOP, CHOP.

FIND A NEST OF
THE MUNKUNG BEE,

CHOP, CHOP, CHOP,
FOR SWEET HONEY.

NOW WE
SHAKE, SHAKE, SHAKE,
AND WE
SHAKE, SHAKE, SHAKE,

FALLING ON THE GROUND,
THE MUNDJUDMI.

WE

SHAKE, SHAKE, SHAKE,

AND

SHAKE, SHAKE, SHAKE,

PICK THEM ALL UP
THEY'RE GREEN AND SWEET.

NOW WE
MIX, MIX, MIX,
AND WE
MIX, MIX, MIX,
MAKING PAINT, WE
MIX, MIX, MIX.

POUR IN KUKU AND MIX
IT AROUND,
DELEK TO PAINT ON
YOU AND ME.

NOW WE
PAINT, PAINT, PAINT,
AND WE
PAINT, PAINT, PAINT,
GETTING READY TO DANCE, WE
PAINT, PAINT, PAINT.

PAINT ON OUR LEGS, OUR CHEST,
OUR FACE, TO GURRIBORRKE WE
PAINT, PAINT, PAINT.

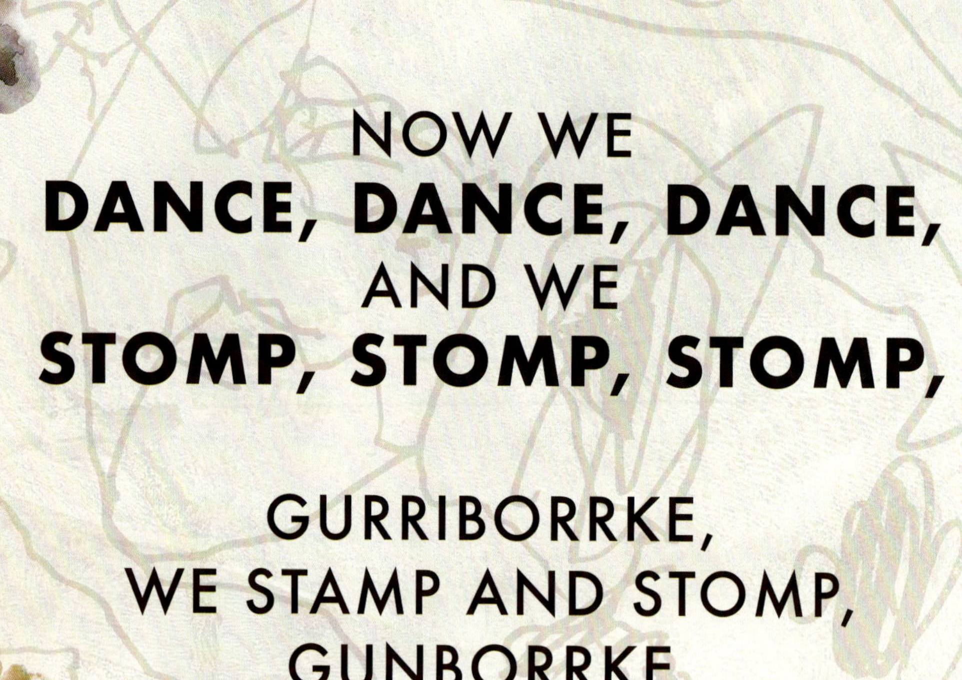

NOW WE
DANCE, DANCE, DANCE,
AND WE
STOMP, STOMP, STOMP,

GURRIBORRKE,
WE STAMP AND STOMP,
GUNBORRKE,
WE ARE HAVING FUN ...

GURRIBORRKE ...
GURRIBORRKE ...
GURRIBORRKE ...

TILL ... THE ... SUN ...
GOES ... DOWN!

KUNWINJKU GLOSSARY

KARRBARDA .... LONG YAM

MUNKUNG .... HONEY

MUNDJUDMI .... GREEN PLUM

KUKU ....WATER

DELEK .... WHITE PAINT

GURRIBORRKE .... DANCE TOGETHER

GUNBORRKE .... HAVING FUN

About the Indigenous Literacy Foundation

The Indigenous Literacy Foundation (ILF) is a national charity working with Aboriginal and Torres Strait Islander remote Communities across Australia. We are Community-led, responding to requests from remote Communities for culturally relevant books, including early learning board books, resources, and programs to support Communities to create and publish their stories in languages of their choice.

In 2024 the ILF won the Astrid Lindgren Memorial Award, given annually to a person or organisation for their outstanding contribution to children's and young adult literature.

First published in 2025 by the Indigenous Literacy Foundation
Gadigal Country
Level 17/207 Kent Street
Sydney NSW 2000
ilf.org.au

Cataloguing-in-Publication details are available from the National Library of Australia

www.trove.nla.gov.au

ISBN 9781923179349

Typesetting and design by Holly Doran
Printed in China by RR Donnelley Asia Printing Solutions Limited